What Readers are Saying

"This book is God-inspired and riddled with scripture to back up the revelation of His word. Gloire Ndongala weaves in meaningful stories that have led him to the insight given in the text. There are "aha", humor, and "real talk" moments that keep you wanting to read more. It is a great tool to use, especially now, to remind us how to navigate the enemy with the Word of God through this extremely fluid time."

-Diane Bardeen, author of Yesterday's Gone, M.Ed., in pursuit of a Doctorate in Education in Executive Leadership.

"Wow, wow!!!!!!!!!!!! That's all I can say about this new book.
To understand the modern days of the schemes that the enemy is using takes real prophetic understanding. This book is written for such a time like today, to enlighten prayer warriors how to be in a perfect position to fight effectively. While reading the manuscript, I felt the need to reposition myself as a warrior. If you really want to have a clear understanding of how the enemy is scheming the whole world today, believe me, you truly need to read this book and it's a must."

Dr. Ansy Dessources

https://ansydessources.com

"A soldier waits expectantly and prepares diligently for the day when he is called to fight. *A Roaring Lion, an Angel of Light* has arrived and Apostle Gloire has given us a detailed battle plan straight from the throne room of our King. He has identified our enemy's strengths and weaknesses, broken down our adversary's battle plan, and done so in a way that opens our spiritual eyes to the unseen world we are currently facing. No matter what point you find yourself in the raging spiritual battle, this book will be your arms bearer walking by your side until the end. The book shifts gears a couple times launching you forward, deeper and deeper into the battle. The final chapter was as unique as it was powerful. What a perfect book for the day and times we live in! If you desire to win the spiritual battle coming your way, then this book is your ticket!"

Donnie Bostwick, Men's Basketball Coach, Oklahoma Wesleyan University

Spirit Led Coach (www.spiritledcoach.com)

"Eye opening! Gloire Ndongala has really grasped what is happening in our country and the world today. We are in an increasingly intense spiritual battle with loud voices of deception on every side. Gloire's book effectively helps us to identify the tactics of the enemy of our souls so that we are better able to resist him and separate truth from error."

Kimberly Winkowitsch, Master of Arts in elementary education, teacher and writer

"With every book Gloire writes, I learn and grow. This book was no different. Gloire has never been afraid to speak God's truth, even if it is not popular among Christians. Crazy right? That Christians would disagree with God's truth? That is exactly what this book dives into. The enemy knows how to pervert the truth and make us become part of this world when that is the exact opposite of what God has called us to be. This book might offend you, but it will convict you, humble you, and bring you closer to God in order to stand firm against the enemy! LISTEN CHURCH!

Britani Overman

Editor

A Roaring Lion, an Angel of Light

© 2020 Gloire Emmanuel Ndongala

All rights reserved, this book or any parts thereof may not be reproduced in any way without the written or emailed consent of the author. The exception is in the case of brief quotations embodied in critical articles and reviews. For permission request, email the author: Gloire@gloirendongala.com

All rights reserved.
Scripture quotations are from The Holy Bible,
English Standard Version (ESV) unless otherwise stated.

Author's contact details:
Gloirendongala.com
Instagram: Gloire777
Facebook: Gloire Emmanuel Ndongala

ISBN: 978-1-7334909-9-3

Published by,
Gloire Emmanuel Ndongala

Table of Contents

Chapter One: Awakening ……………………………………….. 8

Chapter Two: Angels ………………………………………….. 13

Chapter Three: The Pride Inside …………………………….. 21

Chapter Four: The "I Wills" of Satan ……………………….. 30

Chapter Five: A Roaring Lion ……………………………….. 36

Chapter Six: An Angel of Light ……………………………… 43

Chapter Seven: Devil ………………………………………….. 51

Chapter Eight: Twisted Truth About Unity ………………........ 58

Chapter Nine: Grace and Truth ……………………………… 66

Chapter Ten: Satan's Final Destination …………………….. 71

Bibliography …………………………………………………. 76

Chapter One

Awakening

There are many ways to wage war, as we are quickly finding out in an ever-technologically advancing world. Modern warfare, although still war, is nothing in comparison to what was going on even eighty years ago. The tactical strategies have changed, but the goal is the same: *destroy your enemy.*

Similarly, in a spiritual sense, Christians are also warring right now (Ephesians 6:12). The war, unbeknownst to many, is against the devil. The devil has his own tactics that he uses in this war against humanity, with the singular goal of destroying us. The Bible calls his tactics *schemes*. Paul writes when addressing the conflict that was going on Corinth,

> *"Anyone you forgive, I also forgive. And what I have forgiven—if there was anything to forgive—I have forgiven in the sight of Christ for your sake, so that Satan might not outwit us. For we are not unaware of his schemes"* (2 Corinthians 2:10-11, NIV).

The word "scheme" in Greek is *methodeía*. This word has an interesting connotation. It is, in a way, depicting a direction, "a way of search after something, an inquiry; a method."[i] Simply stated, it is a devised, evil plan bent on leading someone to destruction.

The devil does not randomly attack, he plots his attacks beforehand, and one of the worst things a believer can do is be unaware of the attacks of the enemy.

In 2020, the world forever changed. Many will remember the virus called COVID-19. This virus was not the worst virus to ever strike humanity, but the lack of warning when it struck made many people vulnerable to being killed by it. Fear took precedence over common sense, so much so that hysterically, many people during the crisis bought out all the toilet paper.

When the cause of an issue is obscure, we as a society become insecure. In our insecurity, we lose sight of foundational principles and adopt irrational ways. Being irrational is exactly the state of mind the enemy wants you in. It's easy to be outwitted when you're irrationally making decisions. Faith, in contrast, can seem irrational at times from man's perspective but faith's rationality rests on God's Word.

The fact that Paul makes the statement in 2 Corinthians 2 "that Satan might not outwit us" indicates that the battle has to do with your mind, thus the term "wit". The Bible talks about how ". . . God has not given us a spirit of fear, but of power and of love and of a sound mind" (2 Timothy 1:7

NKJV). One way of defeating fear is having a sound mind. When your mind is disciplined, it's harder to give in to irrational thought patterns.

Fear is not, however, the only method of attack from the enemy. In the Bible, Satan is also classified as the deceiver. John says in Revelation 12:9, "And the great dragon was thrown down, that ancient serpent, who is called the devil and Satan, the deceiver of the whole world—he was thrown down to the earth, and his angels were thrown down with him." The deceiver of the whole world! A fitting title for the cunning serpent.

Deception is rarely known in its inception because it disarms one's perception. Instead of acting as your enemy, Satan poses himself as your friend and promises you the world only to give you hell. The devil does not always come as a serpent. Sometimes, he shows up as your family, teacher, love interest, religious leader, and deliverer.

In light of this, one must understand that there are two ways the devil seeks to accomplish his schemes. The first is **fear** and the second is **deception**. Within these two words derive all of the devil's operations. He is either going to intimidate you through fear or captivate you through cheers. The devil comes like a roaring lion or an angel of light.

Therefore, one must be awakened to the realities of the devil's operations. Awakening in no way means we should become demon centered, rather, we should have a solid understanding of what we are up against. This solid understanding must be grounded in the truth of God's

Word and not fantastical tales that seek to fantasize the devil as "the lord" when indeed he is a created being.

Discussion Questions

1.) What is your own perception of the spiritual world and how did you come to those conclusions?

2.) If you were at the beginning steps of deception how would you know?

3.) Am I too far demon-focused or too far demon-ignorant?

4.) What are the repercussions of remaining ignorant to biblical truth and its application to the spiritual realm?

5.) How does the realm of the natural and realm of the spirit interact? What are the implications of these interactions in your life?

Chapter Two

Angels

To better understand the devil, we must comprehend his origin. He was not always a slithering snake. There was a time that he was only beautiful. A time before the creation of this world. A time when it was only God and angels.

According to Scripture, the angels were created before the foundations of the earth were established. The book of Job is where we get this insight into the creation of angels. After Job defends himself against his accusatory friends and tries to uphold his own righteousness, God finally interjects and states,

"Where were you when I laid the earth's foundation? Tell me, if you understand. Who marked off its dimensions? Surely you know! Who stretched a measuring line across it? On what were its footings set, or who laid its cornerstone—while the morning stars sang together and all the angels shouted for joy?" (Job 38:4-7, NIV).

One-third of the Hebrew Bible is poetry, and the book of Job falls into this category. Unlike poetry in many languages, Hebrew poetry deals more with the *thoughts behind the words*. It does not rhyme words, but it rhymes ideas. One type of Hebrew poetry that connects the thoughts while simultaneously saying them in different ways is called synonymous parallelism[ii].

An example of synonymous parallelism can be found in Job 38. When God states, "while the morning stars" and then afterward expresses that "all the angels shouted for joy," the text is not speaking of two different ideas, but the same ideas asserted in different ways. Thus, morning stars are symbolic of angels. In other words, the angels sang together, and the angels shouted for joy.

The angelic activities, according to this passage, are happening as God is creating the earth, meaning the angels must have been around before God created the world. How long were they around? We do not know, for the Scripture doesn't give us full information on this. However, since human beings were not created until the sixth day, each day before man's creation subsequently benefits the knowledge and insight of angels who were able to witness the majesty of God displayed in creation. These celestial beings were blessed with the ability to be in the first Eden, Heaven.

According to the Bible, there are four different types of angels, and each type seems to have its own specific purpose. Some may argue that there are more than four because of Ezekiel's wheels (Ezekiel 1), but we are going to focus on four classifications of angels, in no particular order of importance, that we do not need to speculate if they are angels or not.

The first type of angel is known as the Archangel. Without getting into any other non-canonical books of the Bible, there is only one angel that Scripture highlights as an Archangel, and that is Michael the Archangel. Michael is only called Archangel two times in the Bible: 1 Thessalonians 4:16 and Jude 1:9. He is mentioned by name in the Old Testament in Daniel 12:1-3 and in the New Testament in Revelation 12:6-12.

His name is a rhetorical question that is making a statement, *"who is like God?"* The answer would be no one is like God! Truly we are made in his image but there are still attributes of God we do not share. These attributes are known as his incommunicable attributes: His ability to be Omnipresent (everywhere), Omniscient (all knowing), and Omnipotent (all powerful). Michael is one of the only angels whose rank is mentioned. His rank would be chief or leader because of the title "arch" which means "first" or "lead" in the Greek.

Part of his purpose is to fight and watch over Israel, especially in the last days. The book of Daniel highlights the relationship between Michael and Israel when Daniel wrote down what he saw in a vision: "At that time shall arise Michael, the great prince who has charge of your people. And there shall be a time of trouble, such as never has been since there was a nation till that time. But at that time your people shall be delivered, everyone whose name shall be found written in the book" (Daniel 12:1).

The other aspect of his purpose is to battle against God's enemies, as depicted in Daniel 10:13 when he rescues Gabriel, the angel. Another place is Revelation 12:6-12, where Michael is shown fighting off Satan and his angels and casting them out of heaven. Even though he battled against Gods' enemies, it is important to note that his greatest strength was not his courage or rank, but rather his ability to rely on the LORD.

We get a glimpse into Michael's reliance on the Lord in Jude 1:9. As Jude is speaking about how arrogant some men get, he states, "But when the archangel Michael, contending with the devil, was disputing about the body of Moses, he did not presume to pronounce a blasphemous judgment, but said, 'The Lord rebuke you'" (Jude 1:9). Jude uses this verse to highlight the strong contrast between Michael's meekness (power under his control) and men's arrogance. As chief, you would think he would have just roughed up Satan and went on his way, yet he neither argues with Satan nor gives any attention to his antics. He simply says, "The Lord rebuke you."

The next angel that is named in the Bible is Gabriel, whose name means "mighty man of God."[iii] Unlike Michael, whose title is before his name, Gabriel's title is inferred because of what he is always doing, which is bringing the message. From Gabriel, comes this idea of "messenger angels." These are angels who bring the message to humanity from God.

Gabriel, the angel, is mentioned five times in the Bible. In the Old Testament, he is found in three chapters: Daniel 8:16; 9:21, and possibly Daniel 10. In the New Testament, he is mentioned by name in two instances, both are found in Luke Chapter 1. Gabriel stands in the very presence of God (Luke 1:19).

According to Scripture, there seems to be a difference in power between Gabriel and Michael. As a matter of fact, it is recorded in Scripture that Michael rescued Gabriel from the Prince of Persia. It is crucial to understand when Daniel writes about the Prince of Persia he is also speaking about the entity behind the man, for no man can stop an angel by his own strength, especially an angel who stands in the presence of God (Daniel 10:13).

After Michael and Gabriel, the next type of angelic beings that we know have no names and are simply known by their description, Seraphim, meaning "the burning ones." The Bible only mentions the Seraphim by this name, in one chapter found in Isaiah 6:1-7. Isaiah is seeing a vision of the Lord and writes,

> *"In the year that King Uzziah died I saw the Lord sitting upon a throne, high and lifted up; and the train of his robe filled the temple. Above him stood the seraphim. Each had six wings: with two he covered his face, and with two he covered his feet, and with two he flew. And one called to another and said: 'Holy, holy, holy is the Lord of hosts; the whole earth is full of his glory!' And the foundations of the thresholds shook at the voice of him who called, and the house was filled with*

smoke. And I said: 'Woe is me! For I am lost; for I am a man of unclean lips, and I dwell in the midst of a people of unclean lips; for my eyes have seen the King, the Lord of hosts!' Then one of the seraphim flew to me, having in his hand a burning coal that he had taken with tongs from the altar. And he touched my mouth and said: 'Behold, this has touched your lips; your guilt is taken away, and your sin atoned for'" (Isaiah 6:1-7).

These angelic beings are described as creatures who have six wings and fly around God's throne room, proclaiming how uncommon God is. It is almost as if every time they circle around God, they seem to encounter something new about Him, provoking them to announce how different, separate, incomparable God is-holy!

The final order of angels in our categories is known as the Cherubim. The word "Cherub" or "Cherubim" has an unknown meaning; however, if one carefully investigates its use in Scripture, there are some hints to what the word may mean. The first place Cherubim are mentioned is in Genesis, after man fell into sin.

The Cherubim were ordered to guard the Tree of Life so that man would not eat of it and live forever in damnation (Genesis 3:24). After this brief mention of them, they are brought up again several more times in the

Bible. Nearly every time they are brought up, it has to do with them either guarding something of significance or near to the throne of God.

In Exodus 25:18-22, God speaks to Moses and tells him to place two Cherubim on the Arc of the Covenant, facing each other and covering God's throne. In Ezekiel, they are depicted as carrying the throne of God (Ezekiel 1). The imagery of God riding on the Cherubim is poetically depicted in Psalm 18:10 and 2 Samuel 22:11, where David wrote, "He rode on a cherub and flew; he came swiftly on the wings of the wind" (Psalm 18:10).

It is in this final order of angels that many believe Satan belonged. An honorable position to be in, near to the throne of God, and in the very presence of Him. Never hungry, never thirsty, never lacking. How marvelous and beautiful these creatures were, and yet, amid this beauty, evil was found.

Discussion Questions

1.) When were the angels created? Where in the Bible can someone ascertain the information on the creation of angels?

2.) According to the author, how many classifications of angels are there?

3.) Who is Michael the Archangel, and what was his greatest strength?

4.) What does the author believe was happening to the Seraphim that caused them to repeatedly say, "Holy"?

5.) What angelic order was Satan believed to be in? What was the role of these angelic beings?

Chapter Three

The Pride Inside

There is not a more infamous angel than Satan. Every culture has its own take on who this being is. Out of all the different writings on Satan, the best descriptions of who he is are found in the Bible. Besides the book of Revelation, Ezekiel and Isaiah have given us some of the best explanations of the origin of Satan and his future destination. In both passages, Ezekiel and Isaiah dedicate a significant portion of their content describing Satan and his fall.

The first passage we are going to explicate comes from Ezekiel. When one reads prophetic literature, two things must be understood. Number one, God is spirit, so He is more concerned about the spiritual ramifications than the physical implications (John 6:63). A good example is when God told Adam that if he ate the fruit, he would die. Upon eating the fruit, he did not die physically, yet he did die spiritually (Genesis 3).

Next, a person must comprehend that prophecy can have layers. As an example, let's look at what God told the serpent after it deceived Eve:

"I will put enmity between you and the woman, and between your offspring and her offspring; he shall bruise your head, and you shall bruise his heel" (Genesis 3:15).

At first glance, it seems like God is speaking to just the woman, her offspring, the snake, and its offspring.

But as the story of humanity unfolds, it becomes clearer what God really meant when he said, "He shall bruise your head, and you shall bruise his heel." God is talking specifically about one offspring, who will indeed crush the serpent's head, but also experience pain as he defeats the serpent. There can only be one person who truly fulfills this criterion, and that one is Jesus Christ. Jesus was nailed on the cross and

"...he was pierced for our transgressions; he was crushed for our iniquities; upon him was the chastisement that brought us peace, and with his wounds we are healed" (Isaiah 53:5).

Therefore, prophecy can speak to the present situation as well as the future outcome of a matter. Both the present and future conclusions are essential aspects of a prophetic word. With this in mind, one must know what is transpiring presently in the text, before going more in-depth and unraveling the different layers of the prophetic word.

Here, then, is the background in Ezekiel 28. Having addressed Tyre as a nation in chapters 26 and 27, Ezekiel is now focused on the leadership of Tyre. Tyre was a city located in modern-day Lebanon. According to Ezekiel, it was exceptionally beautiful and wealthy.

Unfortunately, Tyre became prideful and celebrated the downfall of Israel. It was because of this celebration that God had Ezekiel proclaim judgment over Tyre and its inhabitants (Ezekiel 26, Proverbs 24:17-18).[iv] The pride of Tyre in the natural stemmed from the King. It is believed that Ithobaal III was the King of Tyre during the time Ezekiel was writing. His name meant "towards the idol."[v] As his name, so was his life—a man who did not look to God but viewed himself as a god. He also worshipped idols, meaning he had intimate relationships with demons.

Paul, in the New Testament, when talking about meat sacrificed to idols, wrote, "No, I imply that what pagans sacrifice they offer to demons and not to God. I do not want you to be participants with demons" (1 Corinthians 10:20). The reason why Paul wrote this had to do with God being a jealous God and people being negatively influenced by these demons. It is, therefore, this influence that Ezekiel is also speaking about in Chapter 28:11-19 in relation to the King of Tyre.

Furthermore, it is important to know that demon possession does not simply appear in the New Testament; rather, it has existed since the fall of man. The New Testament just highlights it more. Accordingly, if a person is worshipping idols, they have given demons a significant level of access and control to their being. Indeed, they are possessed.

Therefore, when reading a passage of this nature, a person cannot overlook the spirit realm. One must understand the dynamics of the spiritual realm and its role in our lives. Within this complete view of Scripture, it's unmistakable who Ezekiel is addressing in these verses, for he speaks of him being a celestial being and having been cast out of Eden.

Here is the passage:

"Moreover, the word of the Lord came to me: 'Son of man, raise a lamentation over the king of Tyre, and say to him, Thus says the Lord God: "You were the signet of perfection, full of wisdom and perfect in beauty. You were in Eden, the garden of God; every precious stone was your covering, sardius, topaz, and diamond, beryl, onyx, and jasper, sapphire, emerald, and carbuncle; and crafted in gold were your settings and your engravings. On the day that you were created they were prepared. You were an anointed guardian cherub. I placed you; you were on the holy mountain of God; in the midst of the stones of fire you walked. You were blameless in your ways from the day you were created, till unrighteousness was found in you. In the abundance of your trade you were filled with violence in your midst, and you sinned; so I cast you as a profane thing from the mountain of God, and I destroyed you, O guardian cherub, from the midst

of the stones of fire. Your heart was proud because of your beauty; you corrupted your wisdom for the sake of your splendor. I cast you to the ground; I exposed you before kings, to feast their eyes on you. By the multitude of your iniquities, in the unrighteousness of your trade you profaned your sanctuaries; so I brought fire out from your midst; it consumed you, and I turned you to ashes on the earth in the sight of all who saw you. All who know you among the peoples are appalled at you; you have come to a dreadful end and shall be no more forever""" (Ezekiel 28:11-19).

God says, "You were a signet of perfection, full of wisdom and perfect in beauty" (Ezekiel 28:12). We know that after Adam fell in the garden that all men fell (Romans 5:12). How is it then, he is a signet of perfection? Unless, since God is Spirit, He sees the spiritual force behind the king and is addressing that force. It is that force that some commentaries have concluded is Satan who was the fallen angel. On account of this, there is a lot to glean from this passage about Satan. Let's dissect it verse by verse.

As stated, he was perfect, full of wisdom, and perfect in beauty. He was in Eden, the garden of God, which is synonymous with Heaven. He had precious jewels that formed him, not that he literally was made of jewels but that he was precious in the way he was made adorned in splendor and glory. One can also attest that each one of these jewels do not produce their own light but reflect the light. Possibly, Satan may have started to believe that he was the one who *emanated* the glory instead of *imitated* God's glory.

When God says, "...crafted in gold were your settings and your engravings. On the day that you were created they were prepared" (Ezekiel 28:13), he is speaking of the musical instruments that were built into Satan. "Settings and your engravings" actually mean timbrels and pipes. When he says "the workmanship of your timbrels and pipes was prepared for you", He is suggesting that before his fall, Satan had a significant role in the music of heaven, surrounding God's throne."[vi]

Furthermore, he was the anointed guardian or cherub that covers. By anointed, essentially, he was the Cherub of all the Cherubim. He was created to cover, and yet he now works hard to *uncover* all by shaming them.

Satan was in the Mountain of God and walked in the fiery stones. The concept of the Mountain of God has to do with the dwelling place of God (Psalm 24:3-4). *The fiery stones could possibly represent other angelic beings (Psalm 104:4; Ezekiel 1:13; Ezekiel 10:2, 6,7; Revelation 4:5). He walked in the very presence of God amongst other angels! He was blameless in all his ways until unrighteousness—a better translation would be inequity—was found in him.*

This is important to comprehend. It was not just sin, as if he simply, accidentally missed the mark. It was not trespassing, for he did not only cross the boundary and come back. Neither was it a transgression because even transgressions imply that one could possibly return on their own accord. It was iniquity. Satan had determined within himself that this was the road that he was going to take, and he would not be swayed differently.

Keeping in step with this, God states, "In the abundance of your trade you were filled with violence in your midst, and you sinned..." (Ezekiel 28:16). Here the prophecy connects back to the earthly king as well as speaks to the enemy. Tyre was known for its commerce, and sometimes people can get overly competitive and proud when they're trading and making a lot of money.

This is also reflective of Satan in that because of his beauty, he became competitive and viewed himself as the best instead of part of the rest. It was this pride that caused God to cast him out of His presence and pronounce judgment over him.

We must also be careful not to become overly competitive. One of the works of the flesh is a spirit of competition. In the Bible, the works of the flesh are "idolatry, drug use and casting spells, hate, fighting, obsession, losing your temper, competitive opposition, conflict, selfishness, group rivalry" (Galatians 5:20 CEB).

In no way does this mean that we should not compete, but rather that our competition should not be intertwined with comparisons. Plainly, do not covet your neighbor's ability and view yourself as better than them. For in so doing, you are seeking your own glory instead of God's.

Even though Satan was cast out from the presence of God, we never read that his jewels were stripped from him. His timbrels and pipes, beauty, and wisdom were not taken from him. Satan can still appear beautiful, is still filled with wisdom, and can still create music.

Discussion Questions

1.) Describe the spiritual ramifications that resulted from Adam's disobedience in eating the fruit and compare them to the spiritual consequences of Satan's rebellion.

2.) Defend the position that Ezekiel 28 speaks about Satan and his fall.

3.) Describe the difference between healthy competition and competition rooted in sinful motives.

4.) In what way are the abilities of Satan described in Ezekiel 28 at work in the world today?

5.) Describe the difference between the four types of sin listed in the chapter and discuss which type of sin Satan committed.

Chapter Four

The "I Wills" of Satan

The next passage is found in Isaiah 14. Like Ezekiel, God also speaks through Isaiah addressing the spiritual source of the issue and the future in light of God's judgment. Whereas in Ezekiel, the children of Israel were already exiled in Babylon, Isaiah's writings predate the exile. During the time of Isaiah, God is still warning the children of Israel about the imminent doom that is coming if they do not repent. Yet even while pronouncing judgment over His people, God being rich in mercy, proclaims His plan to rescue Israel and judge Babylon, their future oppressors (Isaiah 13-14).

The climax is found in chapter 14, where God speaks to the King of Babylon and the entity influencing his kingdom (Satan). Some, on the contrary, believe that this is not a prophecy having to do with Satan; instead, it is one concerning the future King of Babylon, Nebuchadnezzar. However, there are some flaws with the view of the prophecy being solely pertaining to Nebuchadnezzar.[vii]

If one reads Daniel 4, they find a story about King Nebuchadnezzar that would contradict Isaiah's prophetic word, if indeed it's only King Nebuchadnezzar. According to Daniel 4, King Nebuchadnezzar was humbled by God but not killed by Him. Instead, it was in this place of brokenness that he finally declared that the God of Heaven was indeed the true God. On account of this, one must conclude that it was not just Nebuchadnezzar who the prophet Isaiah was speaking about but the influencer as well-Satan.

The core of the prophecy is found in Isaiah 14:11-15:

"Your pomp is brought down to Sheol, the sound of your harps; maggots are laid as a bed beneath you, and worms are your covers. How you are fallen from heaven, O Day Star, son of Dawn! How you are cut down to the ground, you who laid the nations low! You said in your heart, 'I will ascend to heaven; above the stars of God I will set my throne on high; I will sit on the mount of assembly in the far reaches of the north; I will ascend above the heights of the clouds; I will make myself like the Most High.' But you are brought down to Sheol, to the far reaches of the pit" (Isaiah 14:11-15).

There are some similarities between the prophetic announcement Ezekiel made in Ezekiel 28 and the one Isaiah is making now. First, both address Satan's musical abilities (Isaiah 14:11; Ezekiel 28:13). Secondly, both touch on the fall of Satan from Heaven and his destruction in front of all the kings and nations (Isaiah 14:12-15; Ezekiel 28:16). Just like Satan had jewels that were reflective in Ezekiel 28, in Isaiah, we also see Satan depicted as someone who **reflects** but does not **produce** his own light.

In some translation, the word for this reflection is "Lucifer." This, however, is not the name of Satan but an explanation of "O Day Star, son of the Dawn!" To better understand the connotation of the name, one needs to look further into what a "Day Star" is. The term "Day Star" in actuality is not speaking of a star in this context, but a planet that arises in the east called Venus.[viii] This planet would shine like a star because it reflected the light of the star. The people who interpreted this passage to Latin called this concept Lucifer—one who reflects light or "light bearer".

Both Ezekiel and Isaiah also speak about the pride that resided inside of Satan. Isaiah expounded on the pride that Satan had. He used five lines, each starting with "I will," that explained the prideful stance of Satan and man. These "I wills" all come from the heart and are a catalyst to rebellion.

The first one is, "I will ascend to heaven; above the stars of God." In a previous chapter, we addressed the poetic nature of the Hebrew Bible. In this chapter as well "stars" are indicative of angels. Satan is saying he will lift himself higher than all the angels.

Next, he says, "I will set my throne on high." He wants to be the king. In this expression, Satan is essentially saying he can run things better than God.

After this, he says "I will sit on the mount of assembly in the far reaches of the north." The mount of assembly is a place of honor in Heaven. Satan is decreeing that he will be honored in God's throne room.

He goes on to say, "I will ascend above the heights of the clouds." In saying this, he is indicating that he will rise even further, and all will see him and his glory. Overlooking that he was already in the presence of God, he covets what is not his, which is God's glory. Committing the ultimate, treacherous sin, he finally says, "I will make myself like the Most High."[ix]

Without humility, we too can fall into the "I wills." (For more on the "I wills" of Satan, please read *Out of Darkness Into His Wonderful Light*, A Study Guide for Identifying and Conquering Sources of Oppression, by Dr. Gary Luther Royer).

Clearly, Satan was not satisfied with who God created him to be. As believers, we must recognize that without godliness and contentment, one will never feel adequate. Paul actually writes,

"But godliness with contentment is great gain, for we brought nothing into the world, and we cannot take anything out of

the world. But if we have food and clothing, with these we will be content" (1 Timothy 6:6-8).

Satan was not content with being the anointed Cherub, who was in the very throne room of God. He coveted what God had and sought glory for himself. In the end, he will be "…brought down to Sheol, to the far reaches of the pit" (Isaiah 14:15). Make sure you are not brought down with him.

In our ignorance, I believe we have sometimes overlooked the devil's ability to still pretend to be good. It is in this neglect that the whole world has been deceived. Personally, escaping from the tyrant, Muboto, in the Democratic Republic of the Congo has helped me realize that the devil acts like a double-sided coin. He pretends to be the head in one place while acting like the tail in another. He dominates certain areas in plain sight while working in the shadows in others.

He is like a roaring lion in the eastern world using terror at every turn. He influences tyrants in hopes to forcefully cause people to submit to his will. But in the west, he appears like an angel of light using media as a tool to elevate his secret agenda. In the west, he knows that if no one believes, he is free to deceive. Acting like your friend, he tells you he is not real and causes you to have misplaced zeal.

Discussion Questions

1.) Why does the author believe Isaiah chapter 14 is speaking about Satan?

2.) How do the prophecies in Ezekiel 28 and Isaiah 14 compare?

3.) What were the "I wills" of Satan and the future King of Babylon? How can a believer remain humble and avoid falling into the "I wills" of Satan?

4.) What two qualities does Paul state will bring believers great gain? What does Paul state the believers should be content with?

5.) What's the difference between how Satan acts in the eastern world versus the western world?

Chapter Five

A Roaring Lion

I was born in the Democratic Republic of Congo back when it was called Zaire. While I was still a child, I recall seeing a special broadcast on T.V. that stuck with me to this day. As this broadcast started, I saw a man's head coming down on a cloud and heard people praising his name. It was almost as if I was in a church service, and God himself had come into the building. I watched as what looked like millions of people gathered just to see him.

On the screen, I saw his last name, "Sese Seko." The meaning of it is "live forever" or "I am forever." I can remember the fear I felt while watching him. I could hear my older family members telling stories of people who crossed this man and were never found again. You could not tell what was true and what was fake. Some stories were about him feeding people to lions because they disobeyed him; others were of him making people rich beyond their wildest dreams.

He was extremely wealthy, which caused some to do everything to earn his favor. However, he was not known for sharing his wealth with everyone. While he was getting richer, millions of my people were starving and dying. By the grace of God, my family escaped his regime and came to the land of the free, America.

Moving to America was a blessing for our whole family, and I truly try to daily cherish the second chance we were given by God. I have realized that not everyone around the world gets out of being under tyranny. I think about China, North Korea, Iran, and many other places around the world where people are truly suffering. If they so much as speak up in these places, they get thrown into concentration camps, and Christians are often jailed and beheaded. Even visiting these nations, you can sense the terror if you are spiritually in tune.

Indeed, in the Eastern world, the devil comes like a roaring lion seeking whom he could devour. Peter wrote about this when he said,

"Be sober-minded; be watchful. Your adversary, the devil, prowls around like a roaring lion, seeking someone to devour. Resist him, firm in your faith, knowing that the same kinds of suffering are being experienced by your brotherhood throughout the world. And after you have suffered a little while, the God of all grace, who has called you to his eternal glory in Christ, will himself restore, confirm, strengthen, and establish you" (1 Peter 5:8-10).

During the time Peter wrote this letter to the churches in Asia Minor, the ruler of Rome was Nero. Nero was born in AD 37, and he literally murdered everyone in his way as he looked to become Caesar, including his own mother. He would take Christians and place them in coliseums and release wild beasts to eat them. He once tied Christians to trees throughout his palace and lit the trees on fire just to see them burn.[x] It was under his tyrannical rule that Peter wrote these words to the Church. "Be sober-minded; be watchful. Your adversary, the devil, prowls around like a roaring lion, seeking someone to devour" (1 Peter 5:8).

Contrary to popular belief, lions do not roar to simply scare their prey. Rarely does a lion ever roar when it is hunting. On the other hand, when in conflict against another predator, the lion will roar to intimidate that predator.[xi]

This is no different from Satan. He knows that for him, intimidation is the key to success. He is hoping to strike fear in you so that he can devour you, so stop seeing yourself as prey and began to realize you are a hunter!

I remember my first hunt with my father- in- law. We were in the mountains, and he shot an elk from about five hundred yards away. I thought for sure it was dead, but he told me it was still alive and hiding in the thickets.

As we approached the place where the elk was shot, the elk jumped up out of the bushes. I stood there in shock. But my father- in -law had a mind that was focused on the hunt, and he charged the elk. This was a real-life example to me of how we, as believers, must be ready for battle focused on the mission.

Peter says first to be sober-minded; meaning be in your right mind. Just like I wrote in the beginning of the book, the devil wants you to be irrational. He wants you to think he is bigger than he really is. But you must stay in your right mind. Romans 12 states,

> *"Do not be conformed to this world, but be transformed by the renewal of your mind, that by testing you may discern what is the will of God, what is good and acceptable and perfect" (Romans 12:2).*

As stated by this passage, the way you stay in your right mind is by first rejecting the patterns of this world. What are the patterns of this world? Everything selfish is directly connected to the patterns of this world. Reject the selfish ambitions of this world like sex outside of marriage, popularity, the love of money, vengeance, sensuality, coveting, and things alike. God's Word is the best tool for changing your mind. Meditation on the Word of God will lead to a transformed life.

The next thing Peter tells the church to do is to be watchful and alert. I believe how to practically be alert is answered by Peter in 2 Peter 1 when he addresses the eight virtues that every believer should put into practice. The characteristics Peter addresses are supplemented faith, virtue (or goodness); knowledge (not to be mistaken with intelligence rather obedience); self-control (giving the Holy Spirit control); steadfastness (seeing time through God's eyes); godliness (being aware of God in every area of one's life); kindness (having a godly attitude); and unconditional love, which only comes through knowing Him. Peter goes on to say, "Therefore, brothers, be all the more diligent to confirm your calling and election, for if you practice these qualities you will never fall" (2 Peter 1:10).

Furthermore, the Bible never says the devil *is* a roaring lion; rather, he is *like* a roaring lion. Meaning, once you know who you are in Christ, you can resist him. This is exactly what Peter encourages the believers to do: "Resist him, firm in your faith" (1 Peter 5:9). Not in Peter's faith or Paul's faith or any of the Apostles' faith; not in your mother's faith or father's faith or pastor's faith, but in your *own* faith!

Equally important, one must realize that resisting the devil does not always mean deliverance from suffering. Peter puts it this way, "…the same kinds of suffering are being experienced by your brotherhood throughout the world" (1 Peter 5:9). In saying this, he is admonishing the believer; he is telling you that you're not alone; press on! Yet this suffering will not last forever, and God himself will eventually "…restore, confirm, strengthen, and establish you" (1 Peter 5:10). The restoration is an eternal promise. Even if you were to die here, you still would be restored because Heaven is your true destination.

This suffering that Peter talks about is something many in the eastern world can relate to. But in the west, being beheaded for your beliefs is still a foreign concept. The devil knows that scaring people in America frequently causes them to run to the church. Due to this, he switches his scheme in the west, and instead of a roaring lion, he comes as an angel of light.

Discussion Questions

1.) How does the devil come in the eastern world?

2.) According to the author, what are the similarities between the devil and roaring lion?

3.) What are the patterns of this world, and how do you overcome them?

4.) What are the eight virtues Peter addresses?

5.) In who's faith are you supposed to resist the devil? What will God do after you have suffered for a little while?

Chapter Six

An Angel of Light

It was in America that I met my first atheist. It was my Hispanic brother Julian's cousin. He found out that I believed in God, and he proceeded to tell me how he believed that God did not exist. The most appalling part of our conversation for me was when he said that we all came from monkeys. Right away, without skipping a beat, I looked at him and said, "You know monkeys eat their own poop, right? And they are maybe as intelligent as a 2-year-old! If you want to be associated with things that eat their own poop, go right ahead, but I'm made in the image of God." All my friends started laughing, and he just stared at me, awkwardly for a moment, before we resumed our argument.

As funny as this encounter was, this young man's thought process reflects the prevailing thought process in the west. By the west, I mean nations that share the ideals of freedom of speech and religion, and they elevate democratic governance over tyrannical dictatorship. Within this definition, one can include Europe as a place that has western ideologies.

Europe used to be a place where Christianity thrived. Now the churches that used to hold thousands have been turned into clubs or museums. What happened? How did Europe go from a place that sent Christians out to other nations to a place where Christian morals are frowned upon?

To answer this question, one must understand the cunning side of Satan. Satan knows that the best way to undermine the belief system of believers is by making evil seem good and good evil. He accomplishes this by masquerading himself as an angel of light.

In 2nd Corinthians 11, Paul is warning the church at Corinth about false apostles. He says,

"For such men are false apostles, deceitful workmen, disguising themselves as apostles of Christ. And no wonder, for even Satan disguises himself as an angel of light. So, it is no surprise if his servants, also, disguise themselves as servants of righteousness. Their end will correspond to their deeds" (2 Corinthians 11:13-15).

Did you catch that? Satan disguises himself as an angel of light! He becomes your friend and persuades you to hate all the things that God loves. If you pay attention to the trends in the west, you can spot the Day Star at work.

Good examples are things like "binary genders;" and although not proven scientifically, all of us are rapidly being forced to change our pronouns. Instead of "he" or "she," it has become "they," or whatever society deems appropriate. Albeit this is not a new movement, Satan has been slowly, innocently introducing us to these things for years. He has used things like our movies, TV shows, and music to move his agenda forward.

He knew many would not have hardly any problems with girls making love, so he started there first. The more room we gave to these things, the more sensual they became until one day we looked up, and gay marriage was legalized. Anyone who disagrees is immediately demonized. Children whose brains are still developing can choose what gender they want to be. What once could have been viewed as child abuse is now permissible.

Another illustration of Satan's angelic influence has to do with social justice. Many in the world are or have experienced injustices. Micah, when writing about injustice, says, "He has told you, O man, what is good; and what does the Lord require of you but to do justice, and to love kindness, and to walk humbly with your God?" (Micah 6:8). Truly, God wants us to bring forth justice in the world. Nevertheless, there is a difference between how the world brings forth justice and how God executes justice. The separating element in the way the world brings forth justice and how God does this can be depicted in the difference between **justice** and **vengeance**.

These two terms can be broken down into two defining words, *fairness* and *retribution*. Justice seeks fairness, while vengeance seeks retribution. This is where the underlying problem of "justice" lies in the world. It is not Gospel-centered, so it does not correlate with simple fairness.

The devil, who is an opportunist, seeks to capitalize on the world's pursuit of social justice. He does it incognito, so he secretly propagates vengeance and deems it justice. But as believers, we must know the difference. Paul, when writing about vengeance, says, "Beloved, never avenge yourselves, but leave it to the wrath of God, for it is written, 'Vengeance is mine, I will repay, says the Lord'" (Romans 12:19).

Who in the '70s would believe me if I told them that one day the most dangerous place for a child to be is in their mother's womb? Abortion is not only lawful; many actually believe it is beneficial. Yet, at the same time, we blame God for cures that have not been discovered yet. Maybe God had already sent the cure through a person who would discover it, and yet we murdered the baby.

The Bible says,

"Behold, children are a heritage from the Lord, the fruit of the womb a reward. Like arrows in the hand of a warrior are the children of one's youth. Blessed is the man who fills his quiver with them! He shall not be put to shame when he speaks with his enemies in the gate" (Psalm 127:3-5).

Look at the poetic imagery that David writes in this Psalm as he calls children arrows, weapons. Weapons against what? The enemy! We must realize that every deliverer had to be a baby first before they delivered people. God sends harvesters to harvest the field as we pray (Matthew 9:35-38). These harvesters were once babies who were allowed to grow up into their full potential.

The Bible likewise states,

"For you formed my inward parts; you knitted me together in my mother's womb. I praise you, for I am fearfully and wonderfully made. Wonderful are your works; my soul knows it very well. My frame was not hidden from you, when I was being made in secret, intricately woven in the depths of the earth. Your eyes saw my unformed substance; in your book were written, every one of them, the days that were formed for me, when as yet there was none of them" (Psalm 139:13-16).

It absolutely could not be more evident than what David wrote in Psalm 139. He talks about how all our days have already been written. In other words, God has already established our purpose. Some may be doctors, others, athletes, mothers, fathers, authors, actors, presidents, kings, queens, and so much more! When we kill a baby, we kill our weapon against whatever storm that will be coming our way.

Although what I am saying is Biblically grounded, many Christians today do not agree with what I just said, especially in the west. Satan has normalized the murder of the innocent. Just think about what I just said. He normalized the murder of babies. But he has not stopped here.

Now, substances that were once illegal are legalized. The name for them is recreational drugs. Earlier, we talked about being sober-minded, but how can you be sober-minded on drugs? How much easier is it going to be for Satan to take advantage of you when your mind is not sound? Hence why getting drunk is a sin. I understand the argument of medicinal drugs, but I am referring to the normalization of recreational drugs.

I can write a whole book on all the things that Satan has angelically slipped into our society. The list is long. But how do we make sure that we do not get deceived by this angelic being? I believe the answer is found in Galatians 1 when Paul is addressing what the true Gospel is.

Dealing with the Judaizers, (Jews who believed the Law should take precedence over the Gospel), Paul writes,

"I am astonished that you are so quickly deserting him who called you in the grace of Christ and are turning to a different gospel— not that there is another one, but there are some who trouble you and want to distort the gospel of Christ. But even if we or an angel from heaven should preach to you a gospel contrary to the one we preached to you, let him be accursed. As we have said before, so now I say again: If anyone is preaching to you a gospel contrary to the one you received, let him be accursed. For am I now seeking the approval of man, or of God? Or am I trying to please man? If I

were still trying to please man, I would not be a servant of Christ" (Galatians 1:6-10).

Paul does not gently rebuke the church; he vehemently corrects them. He even states, "But even if we or an angel from heaven should preach to you a gospel contrary to the one we preached to you, let him be accursed." The best way then, to stay on the right path, is to stay true to the Gospel. What is the Gospel?

The Gospel is the embodiment of Jesus Christ. His death and resurrection! His words that he left through his disciples for us to obey in our hearts. It's not about people-pleasing or following the crowd. One must recognize, in the end, it will not be a popular thing to be in love with Jesus; many will follow the crowd, and the crowd will lead many astray.

Therefore, Paul wrote, "For am I now seeking the approval of man, or of God? Or am I trying to please man? If I were still trying to please man, I would not be a servant of Christ" (Galatians 1:10). Paul knew that seeking the approval of man was contrary to the Gospel. Satan also knows that if he can cause you to be afraid of what man thinks of you or to believe what they say about you, instead of the Word of God, he has succeeded in thwarting your purpose. Thus, it is important to be aware of his accusatory nature.

Discussion Questions

1.) How does Satan make good look evil and evil look good according to the author?

2.) According to the author, what are some trends in the west that Satan has angelically snuck into society?

3.) What is the difference between justice and vengeance?

4.) According to Psalm 127, what symbol does David use to communicate the value of children? According to Psalm 139, when is the purpose and life of a child formed and established?

5.) How can a believer recognize and avoid the schemes and deception of the devil's tactics as an "angel of light?"

Chapter Seven

Devil

In the past, I would find myself perplexed about how Satan caused one-third of the angels to rebel against God. John writes about it in the book of Revelation, and states, "his tail swept down a third of the stars of heaven and cast them to the earth..." (Revelation 12:4). *One-third!* Consider how much that is. The Bible asserts that there are innumerable angels, and Satan caused a third of them to turn against God (Hebrews 12:22). The perplexity of this situation lies in the fact that these angels, who were in the very presence of God and experienced the goodness of God, still decided to turn away from Him.

Consequently, I think it is incumbent for all believers to truly discern what Satan did that caused all these angels to pledge their allegiance to him. Especially since according to the Bible, the next catastrophic event is the great falling away. When talking to his disciples, Jesus said this about what will transpire in the last days, "And then many will fall away and betray one another and hate one another. And many false prophets will arise and lead many astray" (Matthew 24:10-11).

After carefully researching what may have caused the angels to follow Satan and possibly may cause many to fall in the future, I have discovered that it's in his name. The name Satan means "enemy," but the name devil means "slanderous, accusing falsely" in the Greek.[xii] Whether it is causing fear or pretending to be a friend that's always near, the enemy of our soul cannot accomplish all the terror or mischief without his power to slander. It is, therefore, his accusatory nature that is the most hostile of all of his attributes. He makes his accusations in three ways: first to God, second through others, lastly, by causing you to condemn yourself.

Satan falsely accuses us to God day and night (Revelation 12:10). But if you are saved, you should live free of his accusations because Jesus is our advocate. As it is written in 1st John,

"My little children, I am writing these things to you so that you may not sin. But if anyone does sin, we have an advocate with the Father, Jesus Christ the righteous. He is the propitiation for our sins, and not for ours only but also for the sins of the whole world" (1 John 2:1-2).

The previous verses, before you get to chapter two, explain how we should admit our faults and confess them to Jesus so that He will cleanse us of all unrighteousness (1st John 1:8-10). Suitably, John begins this chapter by saying, "My little children, I am writing these things to you so that you may not sin." He knows that in the blood of Jesus, there is complete remission of our sins. According to this verse, it is possible through Christ to not walk enslaved to our sinful nature anymore! Yet, if you do sin, it is Jesus who covers your sin. He is "the propitiation of our sins, and not for ours only but also the sins of the world" (1st John 2:2). By propitiation, John indicates that Jesus appeased the wrath of God on our behalf! Not only ours, but the whole worlds, if indeed they see their need for Christ.

Another avenue Satan likes to use when he is slandering people is other people. I remember living in a small town in Montana. While there, I noticed that the number one problem was gossip. There was hardly ever a time when someone was not speaking about someone else in a negative manner. In the world, this is expected because it is the world, but gossip in this town had even infiltrated the church.

After several years of living in this town, it became easy for me to join in the conversations. Before I knew it, I was actually *participating* in gossip. One day while I was talking to someone, my wife overheard me and said, "You know, you can't keep slandering people." I would love to say I responded kindly back, but then I'd be lying. After my temper cooled off, I could finally feel the conviction of the Holy Spirit. I went to my wife and apologized and asked her to teach me how to be discrete like she was. She sent me a sermon on gossip that literally scared the hell out of my tongue.

The man talked about James 3 and why we needed to bridle our tongues. I still recollect rereading this passage that I had read several times in my life and being blown away by what I was finally seeing. It seemed that though I had read it in the past, it was just head knowledge for me, and now the word had finally penetrated my heart. I was convicted of my sin and repented.

Please take the time to read all of this and ask the Holy Spirit to bridle your tongue.

> *"For we all stumble in many ways. And if anyone does not stumble in what he says, he is a perfect man, able also to bridle his whole body. If we put bits into the mouths of horses so that they obey us, we guide their whole bodies as well. Look at the ships also: though they are so large and are driven by strong winds, they are guided by a very small rudder wherever the will of the pilot directs. So also the tongue is a small member, yet it boasts of great things. How great a forest is set ablaze by such a small fire! And the tongue is a fire, a world of unrighteousness. The tongue is set among our members, staining the whole body, setting on fire the entire course of life, and set on fire by hell. For every kind of beast and bird, of reptile and sea creature, can be tamed and has been tamed by mankind, but no human being can tame the tongue. It is a restless evil, full of deadly poison. With it we bless our Lord and Father, and with it we curse people who are made in the likeness of God. From*

the same mouth come blessing and cursing. My brothers, these things ought not to be so. Does a spring pour forth from the same opening both fresh and salt water? Can a fig tree, my brothers, bear olives, or a grapevine produce figs? Neither can a salt pond yield fresh water" (James 3:2-12).

There are many things James addresses in this passage that are poignant to every believer. If we use our tongues to talk bad about others, we start acting devilish. We fuel the fire of hatred, anger, and offense. Proverbs says that "without wood a fire goes out; without a gossip a quarrel dies down" (Proverbs 26:20 NIV). We must not allow Satan to use our tongues as a weapon against others and fuel his evil agenda.

The last way Satan goes about slandering is by penetrating our minds. He will use either evil words people have said about us, what we have said about ourselves, or his demons to falsely accuse us. He will replay things in our thoughts like "I'm a failure" in hopes we would believe it. In so doing, he hopes that we never make it to our purpose.

But there is hope! The Bible says, "By this we shall know that we are of the truth and reassure our heart before him; for whenever our heart condemns us, God is greater than our heart, and he knows everything" (1 John 3:19-20). The hope is found in knowing that, good or bad, our hearts shall be weighed justly by God. If we are too hard on ourselves, he justly knows, and if we are too lenient, he justly knows.

Resultantly, we do not have to receive what evil is spoken to us by people, ourselves, or satanic forces because God is our judge. This in no way excuses us from being rebuked. It just assures us that God has the final word, so we must not fret about what others think of us. "There is therefore now no condemnation for those who are in Christ Jesus" (Romans 8:1).

When we are informed about the accusatory nature of the adversary, we can walk as victors and help others walk in victory. For the enemy would love nothing more than to separate us from the flock through his lies disguised as truths. If we can keep slander and false accusations out of the church, we will prevail through unity. For the greatest force on Earth, besides the Holy Spirit, is a united church!

Discussion Questions

1.) What percentage of the angels did Satan take with him in his rebellion?

2.) What perplexed the author about the angels who followed Satan?

3.) What does the name devil mean? Have you ever acted devilish?

4.) "Without wood a fire goes out; without a gossip a quarrel dies down" (Proverbs 26:20). How can a person overcome slander and gossip according to this verse?

5.) Why does the author believe 1 John 3:19-20 is a hopeful verse? How does this correlate with our lives?

Chapter Eight

Twisted Truth About Unity

There is one thing I believe that the enemy learned from Heaven that he uses better than we do, and that's the concept of **unity**.

One of the most significant revelations I received about unity was shown to me while I was reading about a demonic spirit in the Bible. I was reading Matthew 12 and preparing for a sermon I was going to preach. In this passage, Jesus begins to describe what transpires when a demon leaves an individual. Jesus says,

"When the unclean spirit has gone out of a person, it passes through waterless places seeking rest, but finds none. Then it says, 'I will return to my house from which I came.' And when it comes, it finds the house empty, swept, and put in order. Then it goes and brings with it seven other spirits more evil than itself, and they enter and dwell there, and the last state of that person is worse than the first. So also will it be with this evil generation" (Matthew 12:43-45).

This prophecy has two meanings: one, it is speaking to Israel as a whole, and two, it is speaking to people individually.

First, let us address how this applies to Israel. The house is symbolic of Israel. Jesus is the one who has cleaned the house, although the people did not believe in him. So, the house, though it got cleaned, was left empty. Since it is empty, the enemy, when he realizes there is no other place to go, comes back to the house and invites other demonic forces and creates a stronger hold than he had before. This is precisely what transpired with Israel. They did not receive Jesus, and they participated in Him being crucified. When Christ left, the nation became even more legalistic and religious than they were prior to Jesus coming.

Individually, our bodies represent a house or temple (1 Corinthians 3:16). When Jesus comes and heals us, we must allow Him to take control of our lives. He can't just be the Savior; He must also be Lord. If we do not surrender our lives to Him, the enemy will come back and make sure that our life is more imprisoned than it has ever been. In other words, if you had been addicted to something—anything—and God healed you of it, but you were unwilling to give Him full control of your life, then there is a huge chance you will find yourself not only back in that addiction, but deeper in it than ever before.

Seeing all of this when I read the Word was very encouraging for me as I was preparing to preach. But the Holy Spirit wanted to show me something that was in the text in plain sight I could not see. I felt like I should reread the text, and as I did, the part about the demonic spirit was highlighted to me.

The demon said,

"' I will return to my house from which I came.' And when it comes, it finds the house empty, swept, and put in order. Then it goes and brings with it seven other spirits more evil than itself, and they enter and dwell there, and the last state of that person is worse than the first. . ." (Matthew 12:44-45).

Immediately after reading this time, the Holy Spirit spoke to me and said, "How is it that these demons are showing more humility than my church body?". Perplexed, I had no response.

My spiritual eyes opened even more to the text, and I started to notice how the demon was so determined to accomplish his goal of destruction that he did not worry about being the one who conquered the individual. As long as that person was conquered, he was satisfied. The text even states he got seven other demons, each more evil than himself. Yet how many pastors would go to another church and ask for help to conquer a city for Jesus? How is it that the demons are more united against us in hate than we are against them in love? This is the twisted truth about unity: whether it is for good or evil, unity accomplishes much!

Look at the story about the Tower of Babel. What does the text say about their unity?

"Now the whole earth had one language and the same words. And as people migrated from the east, they found a plain in the land of Shinar and settled there. And they said to one another, 'Come, let us make bricks, and burn them thoroughly.' And they had brick for stone, and bitumen for mortar. Then they said, 'Come, let us build ourselves a city and a tower with its top in the heavens, and let us make a name for ourselves, lest we be dispersed over the face of the whole earth.' And the Lord came down to see the city and the tower, which the children of man had built. And the Lord said, 'Behold, they are one people, and they have all one language, and this is only the beginning of what they will do. And nothing that they propose to do will now be impossible for them'" (Genesis 11:1-6).

Moses points out that these people were one in every way. They were so united that God came down to check out what they were doing. What God says when He sees their unity is, "Behold, they are one people, and they have all one language, and this is only the beginning of what they will do. And nothing that they propose to do will now be impossible for them" (Genesis 11:5-6). Even though they were coming against Him, God still points out the power of their unity. As a result, God says, nothing will be impossible for them!

Unity accomplishes the impossible! Their only problem was that they were wicked, and the Bible says, "What the wicked dreads will come upon him, but the desire of the righteous will be granted" (Proverbs 10:24). What they feared was being scattered, and that is exactly what happened. God scattered them, and He brought about different cultures when He changed their languages. As long as they could continue together, they would have built that tower. We can learn so much from their togetherness.

Did you know unity is God's desire? It is in His very name! Elohim is plural and the singular of Eloah. Throughout the Bible, God is referred to as "אלהים (Elohim)." Even in the very first line of the Bible, the name for God is plural (Elohim). This is fascinating because God is one, yet his name is plural. The "ים ēm" at the end of the word makes the word plural masculine. For me, there is no more evident example of the Trinity in the Bible than this. He is Elohim!

When He created man, He said,

"Let us make man in our image, after our likeness. And let them have dominion over the fish of the sea and over the birds of the heavens and over the livestock and over all the earth and over every creeping thing that creeps on the earth" (Genesis 1:26).

Notice how God does not reveal this intimate detail of Him being a Triune God until He made man. Prior to this verse, the creation of the world was simply stated as being created by God. When it came to making man, God says, "Let *us* make man in *our* image in *our* likeness" (emphasis added).

We were created by a God who has always been united: Father, Son, and the Holy Spirit. It is only befitting of us to reflect His nature. We must come together as one! There are countless verses that emphasize the importance of unity. God does not just look for an individual because they are unique. He looks for an individual so that they can lead a nation to Him. He is about the people as a whole!

Have you ever found yourself frustrated that your prayers have not been answered? How long have you been waiting? A month? Ten years? 70 years? How about if you had to wait 2,000 years? Jesus prayed a prayer for us to come together two thousand years ago, and He is waiting for us to respond. John 17:20-23 says,

"I do not ask for these only, but also for those who will believe in me through their word, that they may all be one, just as you, Father, are in me, and I in you, that they also may be in us, so that the world may believe that you have sent me. The glory that you have given me I have given to them, that they may be one even as we are one, I in them and you in me, that they may become perfectly one, so that the world may know that you sent me and loved them even as you loved me."

The world will know that we belong to God when they see us walking united.

Lastly, in Genesis chapter 11, we read about how God scattered the people because of their evil intentions. He confused their languages so they could not unite wickedly anymore. Around three thousand years later, people gathered again. The Bible says,

"When the day of Pentecost arrived, they were all together in one place. And suddenly there came from heaven a sound like a mighty rushing wind, and it filled the entire house where they were sitting. And divided tongues as of fire appeared to them and rested on each one of them. And they were all filled with the Holy Spirit and began to speak in other tongues as the Spirit gave them utterance. Now there were dwelling in Jerusalem Jews, devout men from every nation under heaven. And at this sound, the multitude came together, and they were bewildered because each one was hearing them speak in his own language. And they were amazed and astonished, saying, 'Are not all these who are speaking Galileans? And how is it that we hear, each of us in his own native language? Parthians and Medes and Elamites and residents of Mesopotamia, Judea and Cappadocia, Pontus and Asia, Phrygia and Pamphylia, Egypt and the parts of Libya belonging to Cyrene, and visitors from Rome, both Jews and proselytes, Cretans and Arabians—we hear them telling in our own tongues the mighty works of God.' And all were amazed and perplexed, saying to one another, 'What does this mean?'" (Acts 2:1-12).

The first time God gave them a new language, they were confused and scattered. The second time they were fused and gathered. There is coming a day when God is going to pour out His Spirit again, and we will experience a move of God like we have never seen before!

Discussion Questions

1.) According to the author, what are the two meanings of the prophecy in Matthew 12:43-45?

2.) What is the twisted truth about unity?

3.) What did the Holy Spirit reveal to the author about demons and unity?

4.) How long ago did Jesus pray for us to unite? How should believers respond to this prayer?

5.) What are the comparisons between the Tower of Babel In Genesis 11 and the upper room in Acts 2?

Chapter Nine

Grace and Truth

The light never runs away from the darkness. You cannot find a room dark enough to hide a light. No matter how dark it seems, no matter how hard the devil tries to win in the end, he will lose. We, as believers, are fighting a winning battle!

We need not fear Satan because the Word of God says, "There is no fear in love, but perfect love casts out fear. For fear has to do with punishment, and whoever fears has not been perfected in love" (1 John 4:18). God's love toward us is perfect, and it is this love that He has richly poured into us through His son that causes us to not be afraid (Romans 5:5).

Another way to overcome Satan's deception is by abiding in Jesus.

"Abide in me, and I in you. As the branch cannot bear fruit by itself, unless it abides in the vine, neither can you, unless you abide in me. I am the vine; you are the branches. Whoever abides in me

and I in him, he it is that bears much fruit, for apart from me you can do nothing. If anyone does not abide in me he is thrown away like a branch and withers; and the branches are gathered, thrown into the fire, and burned. If you abide in me, and my words abide in you, ask whatever you wish, and it will be done for you. By this my Father is glorified, that you bear much fruit and so prove to be my disciples" (John 15:4-8).).

How do we abide in him? By spending time with Him in prayer. Asking the Holy Spirit to be with us and teach us His ways. By reading His Word and meditating on who He is. The truth will always prevail!

What I have come to realize is that no matter how daunting things may look, there is still nothing impossible for God. One day the devil will be forever put away! The Bible explains that

"the devil who had deceived them was thrown into the lake of fire and sulfur where the beast and the false prophet were, and they will be tormented day and night forever and ever" (Revelation 20:10).

There is an end coming for Satan; he has already been judged, and his time is running out. As believers, we must not fall asleep. We must realize neither the eastern nor western worldview of God can overcome the work of the enemy on its own. There must be a collision of vision.

As I was growing up, I went from time to time to the Congolese church. It was in these churches that I saw the power of God moving for the first time. Their emphasis was always on God's truth. I was one day invited to an Americanized church, and there I learned about a gracious God. Their emphasis at the American church was grace. There is a marriage of grace and truth. The Bible says, "For the law was given through Moses; grace and truth came through Jesus Christ" (John 1:17). Jesus never had one of these attributes overshadowing the other, He always did everything in balanced. He was full of both grace and truth.

Many churches seem to always lean heavily on one of these characteristics of Jesus. Some churches are so focused on the truth that they fall victim to legalism. They become overly religious causing many people to fall from grace because they start believing Heaven is *earned* instead of granted. Churches with more of an Eastern worldview, less democratic worldview, tend to fall into legalism easier. This is ascertained in part through how the devil attacks them. He tries to bring terror to them at every turn, and at times physically persecutes them. Dealing with this kind of tension can cause a more strict lifestyle because for them, it is literally life or death.

On the other side, you have churches who preach only grace. This leads many people to turn grace into sensuality, causing people to neglect Christ's sacrifice. Satan comes in like an angel of light. Diluting the Gospel, he pacifies believers with hedonistic experiences and a false sense of comfort, creating a shallow and sleepy existence for the people of God.

A good example is the book series, *Harry Potter*. I hardly know of an African Christian who would read them. Why? Because encounters with witch doctors and the detrimental repercussions of witchcraft and voodoo are a constant. In contrast, countless Christians in America see no harm in reading the series or watching the movies. For many of them, witchcraft is something you read about, a far-off phenomenon you do not see every day. Words like "good witch" seem to take the bad out of the action.

Truly, we must merge our mindsets. We must submit our understanding of the world to Christ so that we cannot be outwitted by Satan. The Church must come together, both east and west, and be humble enough to learn from each other. When this happens, the devil's fear tactics will not work, and his masquerading will be exposed.

Discussion Questions

1.) Should we fear Satan?

2.) What method of overcoming Satan's deception is discussed in this chapter?

3.) According to the author, what must take place with the western and eastern worldview?

4.) What type of marriage does the author talk about?

5.) According to the author, how do people mishandle grace and truth?

Chapter 10

Satan's Final Destination (Spoken Word)

In the last days, man will seek his own praise, and deception will be rooted from inception.

Nation will rise up against nation, all at the words of our media corporations and politicians.

Fights will break between Caucasians, Blacks, Browns, and Asians.

Natural disasters are imminent; earthquakes and pestilence are just a few of the evidence.

Some of this we've already seen, *look at Covid-19*.

Many will say, "there's the door."

Rumors of wars.

It's all written in Matthew 24.

But there's more.

What I just said is liken to contractions.

The enemy will use several distractions.

People will say they love, yet lack the actions,

Humanity will become even more malicious, especially those who are overly religious.

Abstinence will be replaced by tolerance.

"Peace, peace," they'll say, but destruction will come their way, suddenly in a day.

Many will fall away.

Persecution will increase, the law will decrease, forgiveness will decease.

Evil intentions will be mentioned and sanctioned.

Amid the chaos, one will arise to save us,

He will use anything to win, even the different shades in our melanin—that means the color of your skin.

His words the world believed; you're already deceived.

Lies will be breathed, the spirit will be grieved.

He will proclaim, "hatred is done," and encourage us to march as one.

No need for your gun, love has come.

Crowds will follow this new vision and be persuaded into a single world religion.

They'll follow him, believing he came from the firmament.

He will gladly lead them into a one-world government.

His true motives will be hidden, so he can fulfill what has been written.

Inside him will be Satan.

Because the world is greedy, they'll sign his 7-year treaty.

All will see it on their devices and TV.

Halfway the peace is cut short, he will think he is a god of some sort.

But the Jews will finally realize the lies.

With evil in his eyes, he will seek their demise.

The dead in Christ will arise, believers will be caught up with them in the skies.

Heaven's moment of silence…

The earth is filled with defiance and violence.

Once, we thought we were gods and adopted a rebellious stance.

Take the mark, it's the only chance.

Take it, and you can still play and dance.

"Yes," said those who had no endurance; with it went their assurance.

Filled with the self-confidence, they took evils path, hoping to have the last laugh.

But received instead turbulence and God's wrath.

The earth was plunged into a fiery bath.

In a moment, the heavens will open, all will see Him whom the Christians put their hope in.

Coming with ten thousand of His saints to put in restraints those who lived a life that was attaint.

The world will be in one accord, but He will use the Word as a sword and dismantle all those He was riding toward.

His feet will touch, and the mountain will split.

He's king and Lord; all will have to admit.

He will rule with an iron scepter, and all will have to submit.

And the devil will get thrown into a pit.

This is called the 1,000-year reign.

Pray and hope you make it in.

After the 1,000 years, the devil will be released again to test the hearts of man. This part, I don't understand. He will gather for himself an army as numerous as the sand. How does one just betray the Son of Man? Right the depth of the heart of men.

This time around, fire will come down and consume all those who marched against Christ's crown.

A few people say all that will take place is just complete annihilation. How about eternal damnation?

For all those who rebelled, all those in hell will come before God's judgment seat. They'll be gnashing of teeth. I doubt people will still be on their feet.

For they did not want the one desire that could have taken them higher.

Instead, they picked the father of liars.

Now they will get thrown into the lake of fire.

After this comes a new earth, a new birth.

No more tears, no more pain, no more years.

All will change but remain sustained by the One nothing can contain.

In this place, we will finally get to see God's face, ultimate bliss!

Nothing will ever be missed because we'll know we are His!

Bibliography

[i] (n.d.). Retrieved July 02, 2020, from https://biblehub.com/greek/3180.htm

[ii] Answers in Genesis. (n.d.). Retrieved July 02, 2020, from https://answersingenesis.org/

[iii] Abarim Publications. (n.d.). The amazing name Gabriel: Meaning and etymology. Retrieved July 02, 2020, from https://www.abarim-publications.com/Meaning/Gabriel.html

[iv] Apologetics Press: Christian Evidences |. (n.d.). Retrieved July 02, 2020, from http://www.apologeticspress.org/

[v] Ethbaal Definition and Meaning - Bible Dictionary. (n.d.). Retrieved July 02, 2020, from https://www.biblestudytools.com/dictionary/ethbaal/

[vi] Ezekiel Chapter 28. (2019, May 06). Retrieved July 02, 2020, from https://enduringword.com/bible-commentary/ezekiel-28/

[vii] Daniel Chapter 4. (2018, June 21). Retrieved July 02, 2020, from https://enduringword.com/bible-commentary/daniel-4/

[viii] Day-Star Definition and Meaning - Bible Dictionary. (n.d.). Retrieved July 02, 2020, from https://www.biblestudytools.com/dictionary/day-star/

[ix] Isaiah Chapter 14. (2018, June 21). Retrieved July 02, 2020, from https://enduringword.com/bible-commentary/isaiah-14/

[x] The First Persecution, Under Nero, A.D. 67 - Fox's Book of Martyrs. (n.d.). Retrieved July 02, 2020, from https://www.biblestudytools.com/history/foxs-book-of-martyrs/the-first-persecution-under-nero-a-d-67.html

[xi] *Why is a lion's Roar so loud?* Science ABC. (2022, January 16)

[xii] (n.d.). Retrieved July 02, 2020, from https://biblehub.com/greek/1228.htm

www.ingramcontent.com/pod-product-compliance
Lightning Source LLC
Chambersburg PA
CBHW081507040426
42446CB00017B/3433